WAR ON TWO WORLDS
PEACE ON ONE

ADELE SERONDE

War on Two Worlds
Peace on One

ISBN: 978-0-692-98017-0

Pegasus Publishing

Published by Adele Seronde
Sedona, Arizona

Cover: Oil Painting "Kingship" by Adele Seronde
Photo of Adele Seronde by Toby Friedman
Cover and book design by Jane Perini

Contents

DEDICATION

This book is dedicated to my own growing family, and, by extension, to all the children of the world to whom we are leaving a legacy of both terror and hope.

WAR ON TWO WORLDS

Our Western world is linear:
  divided
      from itself
      its human parts
      and from
      the planet Earth.

Our viewpoint of Mankind
  cocooned
      from nature
      and from our own inherent selves
splits us into two worlds
      of dying truths—
      the soul annexed
      from each.

How co-create ourselves again
  as greening world
      of grasses, wings and fur
      as fin and shell
      as bones and skin?
How curve our one-dimensional lines
  forward
      into circled yin and yang
      into hologram of being?

PHAETON

The four-wheel driver of the mammoth solar cadillac,
Phaeton,
slipped out of gear behind the Universe
and pulled up short. The sun
fell off the sky; the deserts caught him
thrust him over Atlas
to invade the sea. Floodtimes suspended Phaeton
upon a rock.
        And as with others—
closing in upon the work of God
is dangerous.
The feathers of Icarus float
as Phaeton burns the sea.

ARMAGEDDON

Waiting for the whirlwind
      we sit at the edge of the curb
facing downtown
      listening to the dazzling static of lights
      betray their after-midnight message—
            a million kilowatts translated
                  into pre-Prometheus tears.
            Such spindly hands
                before the Hiroshima wave—
a human eye
      caught in a counter-clockwise shell.

We talk to our automotive brains.
We pamper cars.
Each heart transplant
      will radiate half-life
            to an incandescent dawn
and at the edge
the reaper's edge
            we wait
      holding the last complete grain of sand.

FALLING ANGELS

When angels fall
                like Lucifer
we ape their shadows
swinging into counterparts of mistrust
                pride
                      and fraud.
We become illusion
capering inside a superstructured prism
        of our inviolate vision:
                molecule by molecule
                    of power:
        power of our truncheon hands
        our nuclear boots
        our self-absorbant glorifying
                of mammon;
the power   we eat   we drink   we coinhabit
        our everlasting thirst:
                POWER.

When angels fall
                like Lucifer
we proselytize a point in time   in space
        we think we know
        and have become
large sunspots in God's eye.
We offer to a continent   a world a universe
        our vision
        our self-encapsulated lie

that you must be as we
must recognize our god
our lust our idol as yours:
   a place-mask of democracy:
   the golden calf.

When angels fall
   like Lucifer
we reconstruct our genes
in semblance of our corporate-godhead view
   as chemical-clad castrators
      of seeds.
We fire our forests, deflower our virgin wilds.
We allow armed services to puncture whales
   with sonar-ray intensity
       of such degree
   we find them grounded on our shoals
   their brains exuding
   through their ears.
We coat our seas with such oils
       of negligence
   that seals, gulls, manatees, and nameless beings engulfed
     die skinless, finless
     featherless
     alone.

     What white-wall waters
     what Niagaras still exist
     to carry us away
     to store our provenances
       chattels

                                        posturings
                              in barrels over waterfalls
                    to eject us
                    across all borders
                    over lightfalls, stonefalls,
foamfalls
                              underwater
                                        out to sea?
                    What whitewall waters
                    still exist as Nature's exorcism
as hand-forgiveness of Pan
                              to drown us free?

When angels fall
          like Lucifer
there are no immediate souls around
to help us change
                    except our intrinsic selves
                    except the godhead held innate
                    intact
                    intrepid in each atom
                              of each being
                              each living entity
                              each existent
                              and articulated form—
which forces us to search
                              again to search, again   again
for what exhorts, defines,
                              refines and bears
                              the kernel Fire.

GODS

gods
sweep wind barriers
smash chasms
open canyon horizons
grant armistice
multiply stars

rocks tremble
cliffs deliver waterfalls
skies crumble
fall
eagles   goshawks   falcons combat
hurricanes
conquer galaxies

humans die
gods hold majesty

WHO ARE WE?

And who are we, Americans
to howl, outraged in fear
that those illegals seeking refuge
within our stripes and stars might rear

their unchained voices, claim
a portion of our greed?
Disenfranchise us by taking jobs
we no longer do ourselves, feed

their children on our crumbs
and claim security in this land
where we barely feed our own,
or hear our children's cries? Stand

up, Americans! And face what
our voters meant: WELCOME to those
from any land or race, or stature
who need sanction from injustice—who lose

everything but dignity. We hide now
as prisoners within our stripes.
Who are we, Americans,
to deny protection to the hand that wipes

our tears, our sins, our ignorance
away, performs our menial chores
with such compassion? Who are we, Americans,
to wield such arrogance that we shut our doors?

STASIS

In this whole turmoil of duplicit wrath
that splits our nation like a bursting boil
why can we not recognize that spectral oil
is an obsolete obsession, a flagrant path

to power-bolt insanity? When we decide
we are ready to be vomited up as a flood
of cannibal delusions which we ride

complacently on conveyor-belt deceit,
chewing up our entrails, mad cow grist,
then...
        we can see tomorrow's skeletal face.
We can penetrate into our children straight
to the marrow
        to the core-bone with no twist:
and ask:
        do you want to inherit this place?

LIFE-BREAD

To cast a seed—
        some oblique seed of longing—
                into a granite crack
invites an act of such impassioned hope
that we become not witnesses alone
                but growth.

For the granite cliff-face
        of today's obese edifice of greed
                has few cracks—
few schisms where small pebbles of compassion—as gifts—
can gather over time, disintegrate and transform
                into soil.

Our lives need such earth—
        deep richest sediment of earth—
                in which to root.
Each tiny sphere of hologram potential—
the innate substance of each soul—

                is taught to bloom.

IN THIS NEW AGE

When will wild animals speak to me
       in the language
       and colors of trust?
Will they search in my hand for a tribute?
Will they fasten my heart to a crust
       of silent darkness
       unfolding
       of waters refracting
moon's voice?
Will my innermost forest lens listen
to purred happiness
describing its choice?

Rupture

How can we allow the secret men
to tear out all the heart aortas
         of the universe?
They hide in uniform—no matter what the mask—
         and sacrifice
         for power or gain
the living breath
veins, guts or bones of creatures.

These whales with ruptured inner ears
that we see dying on every forlorn beach
         of all mankind
because a sonar blast
(the Navy's newest probe to scout a submarine)
has catacombed the oceans
         with bayonets of sound
         to impale
each fish each seal or walrus
         or swimming man
upon atomic cloud of audial shriek—
these are the amputated shadows
         of our souls.

POACHERS

They come at night in bush jeeps
to mutilate the last remaining elephant
in each small herd
at dawn
for ivory.
Bazooka, rifle, canon, random shots
and as it falls—
        the elephant
                still living—
strong machetes hack out both his tusks
from living roots.
The jackals of the forest feast
amid the flies.
The jackals of the jeeps depart
        to soon return.

SPHINX-MOTH EXODUS

I found two moths
lying in the gutter—
their wings outspread, antennae crushed.
Another fluttered down, dismembered. It died.
  Where do they come from, these stripe-winged moths?
  What winds betrayed them to their asphalt deaths?

Back on the road
three live moths hit my car.
A whole parade, cascade of wings
flew mindlessly into the windshield.
  From what burnt habitat, what charred home
  do they flee, out of which nightmare dream?

Are they the signs,
forerunners of a time
when all refugee homeless, torn creatures
of nature will fly into the dark windows
  of our hearts? Do their zebra stripes imprison
  our guilt? Do our own lost wings congeal?

Where do they come from,
small creatures of the night?
Are they only migrating north?
If so, why have I never seen them before?
  Are they the sphinx-moth ghosts of souls
  that haunt our vision?
    Will we next meet in Hell?

The Proud Whales Die

The proud whales die. Which random way
destroys most, we cannot know or say,
for each demands a splitting wide
the dignity of breath. Aside
from which death is worse, another day

is yet another rape of life, stray
harpoon guns exploding guts away.
While our world's blood crimsons the tide
the proud whales die.

And now, new tortures still display
Man's ingenuity; to survey
sea's temperature, sound-bomb as guide,
he bursts all listening ears. Hide?
Leviathan cannot, nor go, nor pray.
The proud whales die.

Eruption

An animal fleeing
        from prescient noiseless shape
the mind rejects
                the heart's volcano
                as it awakens.

A wire of lava incandescent
        in the brain
        a whalesong tuba broiling
                in the ocean's bowels
as yet no formal pattern
        —still—
percussion in the interstellar spaces.

Tsunami earthquakes shatter
any hesitant quiescence—
                prisms blur—
but cliffs are formative
the rhetoric holds
        and finally
        stars and moon in place
                the tides resume a rhythm.

A poem is born.

WHY?

Who are we to linger
        in the harbor of the falling moon?
Who are we to wait for power
        at the cost of plankton
                buried between the wings
                    of pterodactyls?
We are injecting fissionable neutrons
            into our veins.
        We are failing with fused ferns.

Who are we not to interpret the solar wind
        and sail?

WHERE INDEED?

And where is Caesar
          when the moon is falling
          and the tides flow over?
We have Claudius instead
                    or worse—
          perfidious Nero in our name.
This is no longer an Augustian time
                    of rebirth
          where the Muses chant
          and universal tongues are fluid
                    with Pentecostal grace.
No, King Tartuffe reigns in splendor
and his mentors sculpt again
          our very own parochial
                    golden calf.

We are assembled in this temple
                    of sacred oil
          to float our future
          sanctify our greed
          and consecrate our energies
                    to endless waste.
What was once raised in steeple arms
                    as cross
          still slides in stealth to swastika.

No. This cannot be, now, our death.
          When energy is boxed

or circumscribed
it must find exit
         or explode
either outwards as mass destruction
of inherent flaws
or inwards seeking light.

We must find renewed Caesars of tomorrow
                for today
         for solar vision, wind-sheers
         thermal tides and ice-flows.
We must find impacts of the atom
on our soul-heat
to hold the ozone layers intact
and then....
         deliver our crumbling artifices
                into Gaia's arms.

MAN'S IMAGE
(ODE TO CASTRO)

To renew his image as savior
Man must choose—once again—
       an inner voice as bearer
          of a world
that shouts   that flames   that sings
       a new dynasty into being.
He is the King of Shards
          to recreate:
       a Fayam portrait
       a Giotto's saint
             a martyr   prophet   robot
                  of all universal wars.
Like Gaudi an architect—a mosaicist
                      of hopes.

He wears the ghosts of his displaced fears
as emeralds in his crown
       and the opened hearts
          of the vanquished
       form his bones.
He forges the broken weapons of tyranny
                  into rockets
once again: to the equality of Man.
       And he walks
       for a century's minute
             in majesty.

SOLZHENITZEN

Titans are.

In any age

they seek a mindless

inner sun,

a way to speak.

They dance a bridging wire to prophesy,

they scorch the outer eye.

Though blind,

they feel the Stranger

in the catacombs,

in the volcanic bowels

which vulture Death picks over.

They cover Him,

protect His living breath

from future shock, themselves

extended naked

on the rock.

LOOKING BACK TO POTENTIAL AWAKENING WITH OBAMA

I

And is Nehru here today
        in this subcontinent of greed
        taking his turn?
Has he listened for the empire's
        mortgaged power
           to fall
        by trumpet blast?

Yes, now it is apparent
        he is here.
He did not wait
        for sand—on which the fortresses were built—
           to shift
        that he might sing—
he led an untrained army
           of the spirit
        rising in a million arms
        that lifted their silent wing-thrusts
           out of night
to face—across this continent
        of half-awakened, half-demolished monoliths—
           the dawn of coming.

II

And he is asking us now—our Nehru—
(he who is delivering us, despite ourselves,
       from empires of illusion—)
to rise up and STAND.

He is saying "stop riding hobby-horses
of presumption that *we* own the world—
       White Knight mockery—
get off and WALK!"

He adds "we still have Saharas
       of the mind to cross
             but miracles of manna
live
       at the green heart
             of our awakening.

Now - like Eleanor

Who today is life's necessary princess
     of whole truth?
Who can walk fearlessly among the threats
     of being arrested, homeless
     unprotected by law
     deported
and stand upright still, with outstretched arms
asking us to embrace each other—NOW—
     like Eleanor.

Who accepts the necessary new advocacy roles
     of women today?
They have already championed talk and marching
     and, on occasion, trumped
     male opportunists—
     in forms of inappropriate
rivalry. For there is little time and much to change:
queens need strong kings to fight injustice—NOW—
     like Eleanor.

We need archetypal Families again, not only
     Mothers of Earth
but Father Sky Kings to serve and hold
     this world of orphaned children—
     future mind-cells—
     in a process of growth—
a visceral prelude to creation, to breathing truth
and standing high, undaunted, with outstretched arms—
NOW—
     like Eleanor.

To Heal

The illness of humanity
       is NOW.
It resides in the process
of envisioning power
       as life's crown
       in the advanced kingdom
of ever-consuming wealth.
How cleanse cancer of the soul?

Let me start again to heal
       NOW.
Look to tomorrow's child.
He or she is embodiment
       of life's hope
       to rescue Earth
from Mankind's shriveled heart.

How make a choice of futures?
Clean out root evil
       Now—
or die ground into one's marrow,
soul and heart-core.
       Choose your child's
       innate desire
for root-beauty's wealth of happiness.
How? Become again clairvoyant love's
       own sight.

DEATH

Do I think of death often?
Not much.
Not like my friend with Parkinson's disease, who
                barely moving, breathing—stopped—
but answered with precision
when I asked "what are you really thinking now?"
                "I think of death."

No, not much do I think of death.
Not as a poem of lightning—struck—in memory
          for self-immolated Tibetans.
No, not as fire pillars whirling over red Sahara sands
               or dying refugees from famine, warfare, strife
                  or simply root neglect.

No, not as epitaph to mind-murder
          we Americans inflict on countless poor,
          intransigent children, women,
          nameless creatures that live—
or indomitable souls who try to carry
          democracy's failing name.

I think of death
inside the Earth,
our hallowed Earth of Gaia
with daisies as white witness
          to her dying.

SHEDDING

It is time. No one can elect
his moment
      when the light that cradles
fire and bone is gone.
The very guts must spit out
obsolete thoughts
      responses, denial
and stasis of the heart. A dawn
must grow in yearning
for a moving sun
      and all the flesh must call
for life-blood's waters—
huge groundswell breaking waves
      to cleanse dry hearts.
It has begun
and may the falling freshness
      of tomorrow
      wash our lives.

SHADOW SNOW

Why, when the graying light
        is falling
and silence walks in white
do we still feel the sibilant thrust
        of lost streams
beneath glaciers, dark in blue tunnels
        of opaque night?

These etched trees, silhouette tracings
        on ice
hold transparency close, and stand guardian
to whispers of cloud forms which leach
        out blind stars
in the shuttered soft blankness
        of night's reach.

Where is this quietness leading
        our wonder?
How in this cushioned embrace
of all absence of color, fragrances
        or outlines
can our eyes determine direction,
our hearts define awakening
        into the new spring's grace?

A PRAYER FOR GUARDIANS

This night is long, is half time over.
I cry out for all the breakages
                            of mission
              qualities of vision lost
              in a lapse of stasis time.

It is not that I feel less important
              the need for gardens—worldwide
for a passionate breath of green
                            soughing through the fragrant air
              into lungs across the universe.
              That need *is* total—
                            but I crave Your presence.

I do see shadowed sun and leaves
branching into heart-rooms,
              upturned earth as mulch
              as wood-spliced breathings
              composted feelings, hearts and hands—
                            this is my life—
but still, holding onto love soil,
              here in this half-time border of dawn
                            I kneel to You.

You, Lord of sunrise, catch my bent thoughts,
              ambitions, dreams
              trickling into earth
                            for I need help.

I know these gardens are sacred,
        they are, after all, microcosms
                        of Your sacred Earth—
but the whole Earth is holding outstretched arms
        for succor of Your grace!

We must find tall guardians
                for this fragile green:
those gardeners of the spirit
        whose lives are opening smiles,
those other keepers of reprieves
                        within their bones.

These guardians are mentors
        of Your vision to heal
        to hold the Light
                between the filaments of blood
        that spiral as tendrils
                to the blessed
                to the damned
                        to the Holy Fools of passion...

We must reach across chasms of dark fire
                to their hands
                a thousand guardian hands—
                        to form a forest.

Ransom

My heart is not for ransom.
It must free long syllables, loosten
        words of conscience.
For our children in jeopardy of survival
        I must speak.

America's ignorance is fraudulent.
We are a nation in denial
        incarcerating minds
and lifeforms, soils and oceans—Earth itself
        in graying cement.

Some children, steeped in anger,
shoot at stars, each other, practice
        bigotry on wisdom
while others with adults wallow in luxuriance, stealth
        and animosity.

How do we cauterize flames,
the smoke of injustice so thick
        as to be leathal?
Clear stasis! Shout out from hearts and handholds—
        MOVE!

WHERE ARE OUR CHILDREN?

Where are the children of my bones and blood?
The children of my mind gardens—
             are they here?
Do they still extend long-reaching tendrils
             to the Earth?
Do they ask if stars still sing in Eden?
Bathe in luminosity
             of Light's image?
Do their gardens still echo
emerald breath of stillness around
             the chakra mind-seeds
             of heart?

And the homeless waifs of randomness—leaning
against the outer realms of wisdom—
             are these mine as well?
Do these children of world's malfeasance
listen to their sea-waves' cresting
             on the shore,
on the shore of soul's resilience?
Do they hear a flute-note query
piercing through dysfunction
             to their heart?

SPEAK!
(HOW COMMUNICATE WITH THE YOUNG?)

How can I speak to today's children?
What can I say?
       I need to hear, to listen, to wait—
       first, be quiet.
Theirs is another language I do not yet feel.

Can I be like those elders of native tribes
who say "Listen!
       We need to share our world's heart!
       Unless we make time
to hear our ancestors, how will we ever know
       our past?"

I know they have things to ask too.
Like: "Who are you?
       What do you believe? Who am I?"
       First, be quiet.
Do they see truth in anything we do?

Still—whatever the language not heard—
there is joy in a smile.
       A hand touch or fragrance
       or color
       trancluscent in beauty
can ignite fire in our souls.

CHILD

What is this child
but a moment out of time
when dazzling sun-wash on waves
of an incoming tide
echoes
in each star-flecked eye
of this being
in wild splashes of hands
of bent feet—and
of laughter.

COME!

Children of the dying earth, come!
See how our breath is opening out freely—
        to chaos!
Welcome the random particle waves of physics—
treasure the poetry of the unknown—
the untried melodies of hope!

Hope that exists beyond reason, beyond delusion
and trumpeting greed—
        is rife.
It is fragrance of earth opening to rain—
to the deep breath of freedom
renewing itself as whole.

We are all children in our innocence
of what marvels unexpected happenstance surprise
        can be!
We are all creatures of Nature's world, the Living Earth.
Mankind of kings, of beggars, fools and wise.

We are truth's prophets, harlots, knaves
        and lovers of live beauty
        in the core,
motivated by curiosity
with desire, heart-fire and patience—
        to know.
So come to find patterns of loving
        in time's vacuum!
Vacuum of chaos!
Come!

SHE LISTENS...

How can one really know a person
        from one chance pause in time
        one meeting of predetermined choice?
Perhaps very little:
        A voice with trained inflections
        and tonal beauty?
        A portly shape, quite large
        but not ungainly?
        A modesty harmonious
        with quiet power?

                Ah no.
                I feel her love as motion.

She listens to the long, unfinished songs
        of each child's vision,
        the silver thrush-notes of the deaf
        (her own deaf child long gone)—
        the flaming prisms of the blind.
We are in each imprisoned child.
        She catalyzes the means to freedom
            the way of legend.

                Yes.
                I have known in her
                all of the dream-souls
                of our lives.

OLD WOMEN

Yours are the ancient cantos
        of volcanoes
erupting in the Gaia-fold earth.
Yours are the deep womb's screaming
        for opening to birth!

The time of believing in being born again
        is here—
here in the depths of ignorance, death
of falsehood's power, of greed, of deep delusion—
        there is new breath.

Yours are whole symphonies
        of dreams.
of music that informs, invades each new-born heart.
Yours are the wisdoms of reconnected love—
        not life apart.

LEONARD COHEN

He was an old man.
He was a Jew.
He sang undiluted wisdom
To me and you.

He caught the light
Of stars, of sun
To be rolled in atonal magic
Begun

In his unruly heart.
He flung the notes out
To the cliffs, the skies
Talking about

The sound of sea-waves
Unfurled
Away from the harsh Bedlam
Of our world.

We are the human sands
Filtering time
Listening to his spearhead words
In rhyme

With death.
Unless we breathe
incandescent fire
Of his loving
We too will succumb. Admire

How this old man's clarion
trumpets spark—
leaving indelible sunstrokes
In our dark.

WILDERNESS OF HOPE

Today—
tall cleansing storm clouds
have swept away horizons of black anger—
          exposed—
new freshly washed green sentinels
          of hope.

          Is there
time for reprieval
by unsolicited pleasure in blue heavens rampant
          with freely moving breath?
In highly charged redeeming particles
          of hope?

          Yes.
Transient waters of stillness—
azure, cobalt and ultramarine colors
          of blue happiness—
          lie dormant—
waiting in each natural creature's
wilderness of soul—for love's beacon-call
          of hope.

THE TURNING

As the world turns
tomorrow is today.
The promise igniting hearts
is spirit-fire's
white light:
absorber of colors, beliefs,
encompassing growing forces
of green leaf-light:
emerald meadows of grace.
It sings voices
of peace,
speaks in mind's waters
of cleansing,
tumbling through
hope's waterfalls
to mind's sea.

This is the moment
of heart presence—
shifting world's balance
from self-righteous greed-power
to force of the universe
of stars.
It allows the turning
to co create
with all life's living creatures
a hologram
of transcendant Gaia.

Even Today...

Each child
    is that part of a circle
    of truth
awakening in its own spiral climb
    to an apex
    of enchantment.

Each child
    has an infinity
    of means
to explore the colors of existence
    of small wonders
    that share or sharpen
    life's pageant.

Each child
    is a clarion note—a root-tone
    uniquely derived
from resonance that resounds and connects
    mankind's living music
    with light.

BEFORE CONFRONTATION

What can we do but try?
Try to use tears
      as running heart-flow aquifer
      to each separate child
      or creature that exists
            in solitude—
            in misery—
            in glory.

What can we do but try
to exchange
      uncontained anger
      of tyrant's words or swords
      or swollen ego
            with unrecorded smile
            with some small unsuspected act
            of outreach.

Facing fear of whomever's shadow
of hatred
      is not only hopeless
      but an unappreciated weight.
      How did the monoliths
            of Stonehenge
            of Easter Island—
            or imagination's prophets—

become lifted from point zero's floor
to unimaginable heights?
>What lever used?
>What rhythms of singing
>charged each aching limb
>with power
>with supernatural dimension
>of grace?

What can we do but try?
To repair broken towers
>of latterday Troy
>of Babylon
>or fabled twin-towers
>of Manhattan
>>is mankind's perennial choice.
>>It is also his renewed opportunity
>>to rebuild wisdom
>>from spirit's cosmic powers
>>>of grace.

AND NOW- - -

What keeps last spirit moving—
       when mind evades us
       bodies rebel—

is Light
is inner light
       glistening
       inside the dark aquifers
            of soul?

We retain these remnants of existence
       as glowing forces
       as multiple mosaics
of hope
in holding high
       our torn fragments
       as luminous tesserae
            of soul.

We are still here and moving
       in a thousand dreams
       of sharing our children's
desire
to sing canticles
       of gratitude
       for arts' magnificence
            of soul.

SURPRISES

Those hidden well-springs
those echoes of light
        that reverberate
        with emerald
and fire-opal laughter, that kindle night

inside the mind into flame—
these purring smiles
        that stroke the heart,
        or small fragile beings:
a broken-winged bird, unkempt child,

any lost creature staggering,
reaching out to one's hand—
        these are jagged encounters,
        heat-lightning
shimmering above the vulnerable land

of heartache. Also quiet
among tall, wind-filled pines
        are places of utter solitude
        where finger-deep mulch
charms memory with fragrance, refines

each earth-scent into a life
of dark stillness, into eyes
        behind bone. Water music
        that sings, colored poetry

of turned leaves, these are surprises
that leap on our runaway longings
and jump into wild
        yellow, flower-strewn fields.

        There is a language
of wonder in the half-hidden laugh of a child
that awakens us, lost in the womb
of all time. Our earth
        seen from deep space
        is a hologram of heaven.
It is a nurturer and killer. It presides at my birth.

PRAYER OF GREEN

I pray that I will become child enough
to know my heart as if it hung
  sky's mirror,
then turned emerald green with happiness
   spun field-wise
   screened through prisms of leaf?
   It would demean life
not to welcome such clamorous wild joy
into my whole being—in such a verdant array!

I pray that I will become imbued
with child's innocence to know beyond light
   the nebulae
of star-glow echoing God's will
   that enhances
all mankind's life with His music! How
not to welcome such clamorous wild joy
   into my whole being?

Villanelle to the Green

Where is a garden of wisdom where lost people can meet,
so deep in the green-etched fragrance of wind-blown flowers
that we offer our fragmented souls, becoming complete?

Is there a garden of pleasure so replete
with happiness that we make of lost minutes verdant and
burgeoning hours?
Where is a garden of wisdom where lost people can meet?

Wise persons seek shadows of silence to deflect the heat
of bruised egos, of anger. We so need fire-quenching showers
that we offer our fragmented souls, becoming complete.

So much talent is wasted, resources, courage. Defeat
becomes watchword, isolation divests and devours.
Where is a garden of wisdom where lost people can meet?

We create urban deserts in our minds, in our lives, in our streets.
Are there forests of lovelight so resplendid in green powers
that we offer our fragmented souls, becoming complete?

As sun ministers to earth as a life-force, we greet
its radiance in us; as heart-green healing it empowers.
Here is a garden of wisdom where lost people can meet.
We offer our fragmented souls, and become complete.

PEACE

I

Is peace our transient snowfall
covering vast peaks
        of our intolerance?
Do we also bury underlying fields—
the forests, swamps and byways
        of disaffection—
and neglect all living creatures—
        with our white indifference?

Perhaps, alternatively,
snowflakes of the dazzled soul
        do actually seep
into our unsuspecting hearts
allowing us a dawn of freshened hopes
        a gold-edged radiance
                                        where
we actually act in harmony.

II

        It seems
    the way to rein
    the trampling Biblical
            pale horse,
    the way to fill
    extended gaping beaks

                    of fledgling greeds
                    the way to topple
towering Babel's grasp of God
                    might be

             to give to peace
                    winged Pegasus
                           to fly!

                    III

Peace is not a tranquil being
nor is she docile.
She has not arrived at cessation
             of hostility
through random choice
of all man's usual ploys.
No. She has come to celebrate—
to make
             a cathedral of the mind;
to build up, stone by stone
the walls, flying buttresses of prayer
the stained glass contexts
             wherein
soul may thrive.

When peace is credible
she bolts as lightning
jolts heart and blood and bones
             with urgency

of passion to create.

Peace:
the need
             the way
                     the means
             to sculpt our life
             from turmoil's stone.

LOVE

To heal mankind—
　　　flame's vision:
a moving light of angel wings
　　　in heart.

DAWN FIRES

I watch red cliffs catch fire
        and spread
orange dawn colors here
and across ranges that sear
        my opening heart and head.

I, too, am awakened.
        I hear life sing.
Leaning on light
in this translucent dawn sky
        I vow, on its presence, to bring

moving radiance of mind's perception
alive
into all corners of earth
with refracted colors of birth
in rainbows that thrive

in archetypal memories.
        My hand holds
whole languages of blood, of fire
in immutable desire
        to feel soul's life unfold.

It is we, not just I
        who live here.
Here in this intricate network of beings
resplendent and interacting—and seeing.

In Love with Raindrops

To fall in love
with raindrops—
still silver circled light
like mutant pearls—
is beauty
suspended.

To fall in love
with ambiguous thought
that suddenly smiles in comprehension
of intuitive gifts—
is beauty
suspended.

To fall in love
with life's lambent eyes
and hands inside my heart
as cosmic charge of dream—
is beauty
suspended.

About the Author

Adele Seronde was born in 1925 into a family of six generations of visual artists and poets, community leaders. She is an accomplished painter, poet and community activist who exhibited paintings in galleries across America and in Italy, and has published or contributed to eight books of poetry. Some of her poetry for children are being used in schools today.

Two books of prose, "Our Sacred Garden: the Living Earth", and "Pegasus: with Wings on Fire in Education" are concerned with our contemporary crises of both devastated environments and dysfunctional education.

Both these themes are further explored and expanded in her new book of poetry: "War on Two Worlds, Peace on One". Some of the poems reflect and some project the anger and frustration Americans are feeling as the manipulators of greed and power perpetrate war on our people, our resources and ideals, and on all living creatures. Other poems seek for antidotes, and for peaceful solutions. They are built on her experiences of community activism, helping to establish a citywide program of Arts called "Summerthing"; the Mayor of Boston's Neighborhood Arts Program, (1986-1971): a program to unify the city of Boston after its reaction to Martin Luther King's murder. Later she founded "Gardens for Humanity", a non-profit group to help catalyze gardens in schools, hospitals, retirement centers, on reservations and in urban areas, which is now based in Sedona, Arizona.

These poems try to refocus our energies on beauty, on services, on love.

www.ingramcontent.com/pod-product-compliance
Lightning Source LLC
Chambersburg PA
CBHW060052050426
42448CB00011B/2412

* 9 7 8 0 6 9 2 9 8 0 1 7 0 *